STRING THEORY
MODERN INTRODUCTION

AMIT KUMAR JHA

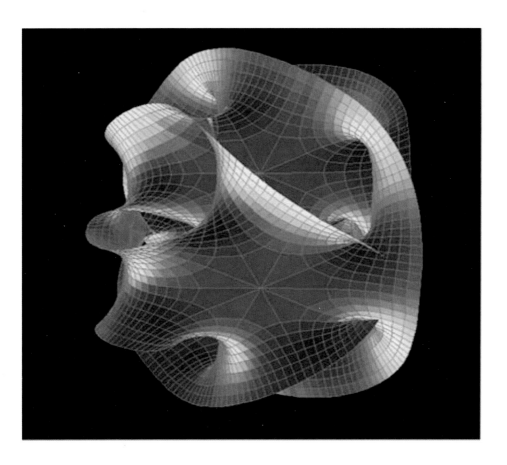

STRING THEORY AND M-THEORY A MODERN INTRODUCTION

String theory is one of the most exciting and challenging areas of modern theoretical physics. This book guides the reader from the basics of string theory to very recent developments at the frontier of string theory research. The book begins with the basics of perturbative string theory, world-sheet supersymmetry, space-time supersymmetry, conformal field theory and the heterotic string, and moves on to describe modern developments, including D-branes, string dualities and M-theory. It then covers string geometry (including Calabi–Yau compactifications) and flux compactifications, and applications to cosmology and particle physics. One chapter is dedicated to black holes in string theory and M-theory, and the microscopic origin of black-hole entropy. The book concludes by presenting matrix theory, Ad-S/CFT duality and its generalizations.

This book is ideal for under-graduate students studying modern string theory

and it will make an excellent textbook for a basic course on string theory

AMIT KUMAR JHA IS A STUDENT OF PHYSICS BY PROFFESSION IN JAMIA MILLIA ISLAMIA UNIVERSITY,

NEW DELHI, INDIA.
CURRENTLY HE IS STUDYING
ABOUT BIG BANG
COSMOLOGY AND BLACK
HOLE PHYSICS. HE IS HIGHLY
PASSIONATE ABOUT STRING
THEORY. HE WANTS TO
BECOME A STRING THEORIST.
HE WROTE THIS BOOK FOR
ALL UNDERGRADUATE
STUDENTS OF PHYSICS T
UNDERSTAND AND
EXPLORATION OF STRING
THEORY. RECENTLY HE US
WRITING THESIS ON HIS

OMEGA POINT THEORY TO SOLVE AND REMOVE THE PROBLEMS ABOUT BIG BANG.

Introduction

There were two major breakthroughs that revolutionized theoretical physics in the twentieth century: general relativity and quantum mechanics. General relativity is central to our current understanding of the large-scale expansion of the Universe. It gives small corrections to the predictions of Newtonian gravity for the motion of planets and the deflection of light rays, and it predicts the existence of gravitational radiation and black holes. Its description of the gravitational force in terms of the curvature of space-time has fundamentally changed our view of space and time: they are now viewed as dynamical. Quantum mechanics, on the other hand, is the essential tool for understanding microscopic physics. The evidence continues to build that it is an exact property of Nature. Certainly, its exact validity is a basic assumption in all string theory research. The understanding of the fundamental laws of Nature is surely incomplete until general relativity and quantum mechanics are successfully reconciled and unified. That this is very challenging can be seen from many different viewpoints. The concepts, observables and types of calculations that characterize the two subjects are strikingly different. Moreover, until about 1980 the two fields developed almost independently of one another. Very few physicists were experts in both. With the goal of unifying both subjects, string theory has dramatically altered the sociology as well as the science. In relativistic quantum mechanics, called quantum field theory, one requires that two fields that are defined at space-time points with a space-like separation should commute (or anti commute if they are fermionic). In the gravitational context one doesn't know whether or not two space-time points have a space-like separation until the metric has been computed, which is part of the dynamical problem. Worse yet, the metric is subject to quantum fluctuations just like other quantum fields. Clearly, these are rather challenging issues.

Another set of challenges is associated with the quantum description of black holes and the description of the Universe in the very early stages of its history. The most straightforward attempts to combine quantum mechanics and general relativity, in the framework of perturbative quantum field theory, run into problems due to uncontrollable infinities. Ultraviolet divergences are a characteristic feature of radiative corrections to gravitational processes, and they become worse at each order in perturbation theory. Because Newton's constant is proportional to (length)2 in four dimensions, simple power counting arguments show that it is not possible to remove these infinities by the conventional renormalization methods of quantum field theory. Detailed calculations demonstrate that there is no miracle that invalidates this simple dimensional analysis.1 String theory purports to overcome these difficulties and to provide a consistent quantum theory of gravity. How the theory does this is not yet understood in full detail. As we have learned time and time again, string theory contains many deep truths that are there to be discovered. Gradually a consistent picture is emerging of how this remarkable and fascinating theory deals with the many challenges that need to be addressed for a successful unification of quantum mechanics and general relativity. 1.1 Historical origins String theory arose in the late 1960s in an attempt to understand the strong nuclear force. This is the force that is responsible for holding protons and neutrons together inside the nucleus of an atom as well as quarks together inside the protons and neutrons. A theory based on fundamental one dimensional extended objects, called strings, rather than point-like particles, can account qualitatively for various features of the strong nuclear force and the strongly interacting particles (or hadrons). The basic idea in the string description of the strong interactions is that specific particles correspond to specific oscillation modes (or quantum states) of the string. This proposal gives a very satisfying unified picture in that it postulates a single fundamental object (namely, the string) to explain the myriad of different observed hadrons, as indicated in Fig.

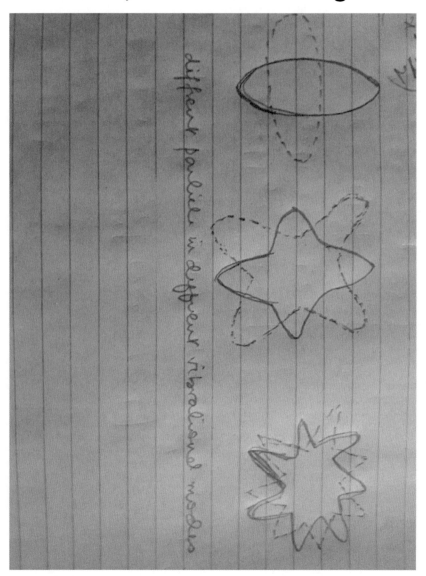

1.1.

In the early 1970s another theory of the strong nuclear force –called quantum chromodynamics (or QCD) – was developed. As a result of this, as well as various technical problems in the string theory approach, string theory fell out of favour. The current viewpoint is that this program made good sense, and so it has again become an active area of research. The concrete string theory that describes the strong interaction is still not known, though one now has a much better understanding of how to approach the problem. String theory turned out to be well suited for an even more ambitious purpose: the construction of a quantum theory that unifies the description of gravity and the other fundamental forces of nature. In principle, it has the potential to provide a complete understanding of particle physics and of cosmology. Even though this is still a distant dream, it is clear that in this fascinating theory surprises arise over and over.

1.2 General features Even though string theory is not yet fully formulated, and we cannot yet give a detailed description of how the standard model of elementary particles should emerge at low energies, or how the Universe originated, there are some general features of the theory that have been well understood. These are features that seem to be quite generic irrespective of what the final formulation of string theory might be. Gravity The first general feature of string theory, and perhaps the most important, is that general relativity is naturally incorporated in the theory. The theory gets modified at very short distances/high energies but at ordinary distances and energies it is present in exactly the form as proposed by Einstein. This is significant, because general relativity is arising within the framework of a Fig. 1.1. Different particles are different vibrational modes of a string.

Yang–Mills gauge theory

In order to ful fill the goal of describing all of elementary particle physics, the presence of a graviton in the string spectrum is not enough. One also needs to account for the standard model, which is a Yang–Mills theory based on the gauge group SU(3)×SU(2)×U(1). The appearance of Yang–Mills gauge theories of the sort that comprise the standard model is a general feature of string theory. Moreover, matter can appear in complex chiral representations, which is an essential feature of the standard model. However, it is not yet understood why the specific SU(3) × SU(2) × U(1) gauge theory with three generations of quarks and leptons is singled out in nature.

Supersymmetry

The third general feature of string theory is that its consistency requires supersymmetry, which is a symmetry that relates bosons to fermions is required. There exist non supersymmetric bosonic string theories (discussed in Chapters 2 and 3), but lacking fermions, they are completely unrealistic. The mathematical consistency of string theories with fermions depends crucially on local supersymmetry. Supersymmetry is a generic feature of all potentially realistic string theories. The fact that this symmetry has not yet been discovered is an indication that the characteristic energy scale of supersymmetry breaking and the masses of supersymmetry partners of known particles are above experimentally determined lower bounds. Space-time supersymmetry is one of the major predictions of superstring theory that could be confirmed experimentally at accessible energies. A variety of arguments, not specific to string theory, suggest that the characteristic energy scale associated with supersymmetry breaking should be related to the electroweak scale, in other words in the range 100 GeV to a few TeV. If this is correct, super partners should be observable at the CERN Large Hadron Collider (LHC), which is scheduled to begin operating in 2007.

Extra dimensions of space

In contrast to many theories in physics, superstring theories are able to predict the dimension of the space-time in which they live. The theory is only consistent in a ten-dimensional space-time and in some cases an eleventh dimension is also possible. To make contact between string theory and the four-dimensional world of everyday experience, the most straightforward possibility is that six or seven of the dimensions are compact ified on an internal manifold, whose size is sufficiently small to have escaped detection.

For purposes of particle physics, the other four dimensions should give our four-dimensional space-time. Of course, for purposes of cosmology, other (time-dependent) geometries may also arise.

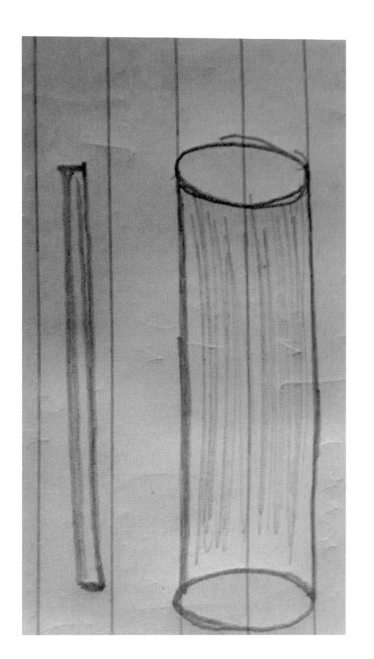

Fig. 1.2. From far away a two-dimensional cylinder looks one-dimensional. The idea of an extra compact dimension was first discussed by Kaluza and Klein in the 1920s. Their goal was to construct a unified description of electromagnetism and gravity in four dimensions by compactifying five dimensional general relativity on a circle. Even though we now know that this is not how electromagnetism arises, the essence of this beautiful approach reappears in string theory. The Kaluza–Klein idea, nowadays referred to as compactification, can be illustrated in terms of the two cylinders of Fig. 1.2. The surface of the first cylinder is two-dimensional. However, if the radius of the circle becomes extremely small, or equivalently if the cylinder is viewed from a large distance, the cylinder looks effectively one-dimensional. One now imagines that the long dimension of the cylinder is replaced by our four-dimensional space-time and the short dimension by an appropriate six, or seven-dimensional compact manifold. At large distances or low energies the compact internal space cannot be seen and the world looks effectively four-dimensional. , even if the internal manifolds are invisible, their topological properties determine the particle content and structure of the four-dimensional theory. In the mid-1980s Calabi–Yau manifolds were first considered for compactifying six extra dimensions, and they were shown to be phenomenologically rather promising, even though some serious drawbacks posed a problem for the predictive powerof string theory. In contrast to the circle, Calabi–Yau manifolds do not have isometries, and part of their role is to break symmetries rather than to make them.

The size of strings

In conventional quantum field theory the elementary particles are mathematical points, whereas in perturbative string theory the fundamental objects are one-dimensional loops (of zero thickness). Strings have a characteristic length scale, denoted ls, which can be estimated by dimensional analysis. Since string theory is a relativistic quantum theory that includes gravity it must involve the fundamental constants c (the speed of light), ‾h (Planck's constant divided by 2π), and G (Newton's gravitational constant). From these one can form a length, known as the Planck length $l_p = \sqrt{\hbar G \, c^3}$ Similarly, the Planck mass is $m_p = \sqrt{\hbar c \, G}^{1/2 \, 1/2}$

$= 1.6 \times 10^{-33}$ cm.

$= 1.2 \times 10^{19}$ GeV$/c^2$. The Planck scale is the natural first guess for a rough estimate of the fundamental string length scale as well as the characteristic size of compact extra dimensions. Experiments at energies far below the Planck energy cannot resolve distances as short as the

Planck length. Thus, at such energies, strings can be accurately approximated by point particles. This explains why quantum field theory has been so successful in describing our world. 1.3

Basic string theory

As a string evolves in time it sweeps out a two-dimensional surface in space-time, which is called the string world sheet of the string. This is the string counterpart of the world line for a point particle. In quantum field theory, analyzed in perturbation theory, contributions to amplitudes are associated with Feynman diagrams, which depict possible configurations of world lines. In particular, interactions correspond to junctions of world lines. Similarly, perturbation expansions in string theory involve string world sheets of various topologies. The existence of interactions in string theory can be understood as a consequence of world-sheet topology rather than of a local singularity on theworld sheet. This difference from point-particle theories has two important implications. First, in string theory the structure of interactions is uniquely determined by the free theory. There are no arbitrary interactions to be chosen. Second, since string interactions are not associated with short-distance singularities, string theory amplitudes have no ultraviolet divergences. The string scale 1/ls acts as a UV cutoff.

World-volume actions and the critical dimension

A string can be regarded as a special case of a p-brane, which is an object with p spatial dimensions and tension (or energy density) Tp. In fact, various p-branes do appear in superstring theory as nonperturbative excitations. The classical motion of a p-brane extremizes the (p+1)-dimensional volume V that it sweeps out in space-time. Thus there is a p-brane action that is given by $S_p = -T_p V$. In the case of the fundamental string, which has $p = 1$, V is the area of the string world sheet and the action is called the Nambu–Goto action. Classically, the Nambu–Goto action is equivalent to the string sigmamodel action $S_\sigma = -T 2 \sqrt{}$

$-\sqrt{h}h^{\alpha\beta}\eta_{\mu\nu}\partial_\alpha X^\mu\partial_\beta X^\nu d\sigma d\tau$, where $h_{\alpha\beta}(\sigma,\tau)$ is an auxiliary world-sheet metric, $h = \det h_{\alpha\beta}$, and $h^{\alpha\beta}$ is the inverse of $h_{\alpha\beta}$. The functions $X^\mu(\sigma,\tau)$ describe the space-time embedding of the string world sheet. The Euler–Lagrange equation for $h_{\alpha\beta}$ can be used to eliminate it from the action and recover the Nambu–Goto action. Quantum mechanically, the story is more subtle. Instead of eliminating h via its classical field equations, one should perform a Feynman path integral, using standard machinery to deal with the local symmetries and gauge fixing. When this is done correctly, one finds that there is a conformal anomaly unless the space-time dimension is D = 26. An analogous analysis for superstrings gives the critical dimension D = 10.

Closed strings and open strings

The parameter τ in the embedding functions $X\mu(\sigma,\tau)$ is the world-sheet time coordinate and σ parametrizes the string at a given world-sheet time. For a closed string, which is topologically a circle, one should impose periodicity in the spatial parameter σ. Choosing its range to be π one identifies both ends of the string $X\mu(\sigma,\tau) = X\mu(\sigma + \pi,\tau)$. All string theories contain closed strings, and the graviton always appears as a massless mode in the closed-string spectrum of critical string theories. For an open string, which is topologically a line interval, each end can be required to satisfy either Neumann or Dirichlet boundary conditions (for each value of μ). The Dirichlet condition specifies a space-time hypersurface on which the string ends. The only way this makes sense is if the open string ends on a physical object, which is called a D-brane. (D stands for Dirichlet.) If all the open-string boundary conditions are Neumann, then the ends of the string can be anywhere in the space-time. The modern interpretation is that this means that space-time-filling D-branes are present.

Perturbation theory

Perturbation theory is useful in a quantum theory that has a small dimensionless coupling constant, such as quantum electrodynamics (QED), since it allows one to compute physical quantities as expansions in the small parameter. In QED the small parameter is the fine-structure constant $\alpha \sim 1/137$. For a physical quantity $T(\alpha)$, one computes (using Feynman diagrams) $T(\alpha) = T0 + \alpha T1 + \alpha 2T2 + ...$ Perturbation series are usually asymptotic expansions with zero radius of convergence. Still, they can be useful, if the expansion parameter is small, because the first terms in the expansion provide an accurate approximation. The heterotic and type II superstring theories contain oriented closed strings only. As a result, the only world sheets in their perturbation expansions are closed oriented Riemann surfaces. There is a unique world-sheet topology at each order of the perturbation expansion, and its contribution is UV finite. The fact that there is just one string theory Feynman diagram at each order in the perturbation expansion is in striking contrast to the large number of Feynman diagrams that appear in quantum field theory. In the case of string theory there is no particular reason to expect the coupling constant g_s to be small. So it is unlikely that a realistic vacuum could be analyzed accurately using only perturbation theory. For this reason, it is important to understand nonperturbative effects in string theory.

Superstrings

The first superstring revolution began in 1984 with the discovery that quantum mechanical consistency of a ten-dimensional theory with N = 1 supersymmetry requires a local Yang–Mills gauge symmetry based on one of two possible Lie algebras: SO(32) or E8×E8. As is explained in , only for these two choices do certain quantum mechanical anomalies cancel. The fact that only these two groups are possible suggested that string theory has a very constrained structure, and therefore it might be very predictive. 2 When one uses the superstring formalism for both left-moving modes and right-moving modes, the supersymmetries associated with the left-movers and the right-movers can have either opposite handedness or the same handedness. These two possibilities give different theories called the type IIA and type IIB superstring theories, respectively. A third possibility, called type I superstring theory, can be derived from the type IIB theory by modding out by its left–right symmetry, a procedure called orientifold projection. The strings that survive this projection are unoriented. The type I and type II superstring theories are described in Chapters 4 and 5 using formalisms with world-sheet and space-time supersymmetry, respectively. Amore surprising possibility is to use the formalism of the 26-dimensional bosonic string for the left-movers and the formalism of the 10-dimensional superstring for the right-movers. The string theories constructed in this way are called "heterotic.". The mismatch in space-time dimensions may sound strange, but it is actually exactly what is needed. The extra 16 left-moving dimensions must describe a torus with very special properties to give a consistent theory. There are precisely two distinct tori that have the required properties, and they correspond to the Lie algebras SO(32) and E8 × E8. Altogether, there are five distinct superstring theories, each in ten dimensions. Three dimensions has 16 real components, so these theories have 16 conserved supercharges. The type I superstring theory has the gauge group SO(32), whereas the heterotic theories realize both SO(32) and E8 × E8. The other two theories, type IIA and type IIB, have N = 2 supersymmetry or equivalently 32 supercharges.

1.4

Modern developments in superstring theory

The realization that there are five different superstring theories was somewhat puzzling. Certainly, there is only one Universe, so it would be most satisfying if there were only one possible theory. In the late 1980s it wasrealized that there is a property known as T-duality that relates the two type II theories and the two heterotic theories, so that they shouldn't really be regarded as distinct theories. Progress in understanding non perturbative phenomena was achieved in the 1990s. Non perturbative S-dualities and the opening up of an eleventh dimension at strong coupling in certain cases led to new identifications. Once all of these correspondences are taken into account, one ends up with the best possible conclusion: there is a unique underlying theory. Some of these developments are summarized below.

T-duality

String theory exhibits many surprising properties. One of them, called T-Duality, is . T-duality implies that in many cases two different geometries for the extra dimensions are physically equivalent! In the simplest example, a circle of radius R is equivalent to a circle of radius $2s/R$, where (as before) s is the fundamental string length scale. T-duality typically relates two different theories.

For example, it relates the two type II and the two heterotic theories. Therefore, the type IIA and type IIB theories (also the two heterotic theories) should be regarded as a single theory. More precisely, they represent opposite ends of a continuum of geometries as one varies the radius of a circular dimension. This radius is not a parameter of the underlying theory. Rather, it arises as the vacuum expectation value of a scalar field, and it is determined dynamically. There are also fancier examples of duality equivalences. For example, there is an equivalence of type IIA superstring theory compactified on a Calabi–Yau manifold and type IIB compactified on the "mirror" Calabi–Yau manifold. This mirror pairing of topologically distinct Calabi–Yau manifolds . A surprising connection to T-duality will emerge.

S-duality

Another kind of duality —called S-duality —was discovered as part of the second superstring revolution in the mid-1990s. . S-duality relates the string coupling constant gs to 1/gs in the same way that T-duality relates R to 2s/R. The two basic examples relate the type I superstring theory to the SO(32) heterotic string theory and the type IIB superstring theory to itself. Thus, given our knowledge of the small gs behavior of these theories, given by perturbation theory, we learn how these three theories behave when g_s 1. For example, strongly coupled type I theory is equivalent to weakly coupled SO(32) heterotic theory. In the type IIB case the theory is related to itself, so one is actually dealing with a symmetry. The string coupling constant g_s is given by the vacuum expectation value of $\exp\phi$, where ϕ is the dilaton field. S-duality, like Tduality, is actually a field transformation, $\phi \to -\phi$, and not just a statement about vacuum expectation values.

D-branes

When studied nonperturbatively, one discovers that superstring theory contains various p-branes, objects with p spatial dimensions, in addition to the fundamental strings. All of the p-branes, with the single exception of the fundamental string (which is a 1-brane), become infinitely heavy as gs → 0, and therefore they do not appear in perturbation theory. On the other hand, when the coupling gs is not small, this distinction is no longer significant. When that is the case, all of the p-branes are just as important as the fundamental strings, so there is p-brane democracy. The type I and II superstring theories contain a class of p-branes called Dbranes, whose tension is proportional $1/gs$.

As was mentioned earlier, their defining property is that they are objects on which fundamental strings can end. The fact that fundamental strings can end on D-branes implies that quantum field theories of the Yang–Mills type, like the standard model, reside on the world volumes of D-branes. The Yang–Mills fields arise as the massless modes of open strings attached to the D-branes. The fact that theories resembling the standard model reside on D-branes has many interesting implications. For example, it has led to the speculation that the reason we experience four space-time dimensions is because we are confined to live on three-dimensional D-branes (D3-branes), which are embedded in a higher-dimensional space-time. Model-building along these lines, sometimes called the brane-world approach or scenario.

What is M-theory?

 S-duality explains how three of the five original superstring theories behave at strong coupling. This raises the question: What happens to the other two superstring theories –type IIA and E8×E8 heterotic –when gs is large? The answer, which came as quite a surprise, is that they grow an eleventh dimension of size gss. This new dimension is a circle in the type IIA case and a line interval in the heterotic case. When the eleventh dimension islarge, one is outside the regime of perturbative string theory, and new techniques are required. Most importantly, a new type of quantum theory in 11 dimensions, called M-theory, emerges. At low energies it is approximated by a classical field theory called 11-dimensional supergravity, but M-theory is much more than that. The relation between M-theory and the two superstring theories previously mentioned, together with the T and S dualities discussed above, imply that the five superstring theories are connected by a web of dualities, as depicted in Fig. 1.3. They can be viewed as different corners of a single theory. type IIA 11d SUGRA type IIB E8XE8 SO(32) type I Fig. 1.3. Different string theories are connected through a web of dualities. There are techniques for identifying large classes of superstring and Mtheory vacua, and describing them exactly, but there is not yet a succinct and compelling formulation of the underlying theory that gives rise to these vacua. Such a formulation should be completely unique, with no adjustable dimensionless parameters or other arbitrariness. Many things that we usually take for granted, such as the existence of a space-time manifold, are likely to be understood as emergent properties of specific vacua rather than identifiable features of the underlying theory. If this is correct, then the missing formulation of the theory must be quite unlike any previous theory. Usual approaches based on quantum fields depend on the existence of an ambient space-time manifold. It is not clear what the basic degrees of freedom should be in a theory that does not assume a space-time manifold at the outset. There is an interesting proposal for an exact quantum mechanical description of M-theory, applicable to certain space-time backgrounds, that goes by the name of Matrix theory. Matrix theory gives a dual description of Mtheory in flat 11-dimensional space-time in terms of the quantum mechanics of N ×N matrices in the large N limit. When n of the spatial dimensions are compactified on a torus, the dual Matrix theory becomes a quantum f ield theory in n spatial dimensions (plus time). There is evidence that this conjecture is correct when n is not too large. However, it is unclear how to generalize it to other compactification geometries, so Matrix theory provides only pieces of a more complete description of M-theory.

F-theory

As previously discussed, the type IIA and heterotic E8 ×E8 theories can be viewed as arising from a more fundamental eleven-dimensional theory, Mtheory. One may wonder if the other superstring theories can be derived in a similar fashion. An approach, called F-theory, is described in Chapter 9. It utilizes the fact that ten-dimensional type IIB superstring theory has a non perturbative SL(2,) symmetry. Moreover, this is the modular group of a torus and the type IIB theory contains a complex scalar field τ that transforms under SL(2,) as the complex structure of a torus.

Therefore, this symmetry can be given a geometric interpretation if the type IIB theory is viewed as having an auxiliary two-torus T2 with complex structure τ. The SL(2,) symmetry then has a natural interpretation as the symmetry of the torus. Flux compactifications One question that already bothered Kaluza and Klein is why should the f fifth dimension curl up? Another puzzle in those early days was the size of the circle, and what stabilizes it at a particular value. These questions have analogs in string theory, where they are part of what is called the moduli space problem. In string theory the shape and size of the internal manifold is dynamically determined by the vacuum expectation values of scalar fields. String theorists have recently been able to provide answers to these questions in the context of flux compactifications , which is a rapidly developing area of modern string theory research. Even though the underlying theory (M-theory) is unique, it admits an enormous number of different solutions (or quantum vacua). One of these solutions should consist of four-dimensional Minko-wski space-time times a compact manifold and accurately describes the world of particle physics. One of the major challenges of modern string theory research is to find this solution. It would be marvelous to identify the correct vacuum, and at the same time to understand why it is the right one. Is it picked out by some special mathematical property, or is it just an environmental accident of our particular corner of the Universe? The way this question plays out will be important in determining the extent to which the observed world of particle physics can be deduced from first principles.

Black-hole entropy

It follows from general relativity that macroscopic

black holes behave like thermodynamic objects with a well-defined temperature and entropy. The entropy is given (in gravitational units) by 1/4 the area of the event horizon, which is the Bekenstein–Hawking entropy formula. In quantum theory, an entropy S ordinarily implies that there are a large number of quantum states (namely, expS of them) that contribute to the corresponding microscopic description. So a natural question is whether this rule also applies to black holes and their higher-dimensional generalizations, which are called black pbranes. D-branes provide a set-up in which this question can be investigated. In the early work on this subject, reliable techniques for counting microstates only existed for very special types of black holes having a large amount of supersymmetry. In those cases one found agreement with the entropy formula. More recently, one has learned how to analyze a much larger class of black holes and black p-branes, and even how to compute corrections to the area formula. Many examples have been studied and no discrepancies have been found, aside from corrections that are expected. It is fair to say that these studies have led to a much deeper understanding of the thermodynamic properties of black holes in terms of string-theory microphysics, a fact that is one of the most striking successes of string theory so far.

AdS/CFT duality

A remarkable discovery made in the late 1990s is the exact equivalence (or duality) of conformally invariant quantum field theories and superstring theory or M-theory in special space-time geometries. A collection of coincident p-branes produces a space-time geometry with a horizon, like that of a black hole. In the vicinity of the horizon, this geometry can be approximated by a product of an anti-de Sitter space and a sphere. In the example that arisesfrom considering N coincident D3-branes in the type IIB superstring theory, one obtains a duality between SU(N) Yang–Mills theory with N = 4 supersymmetry in four dimensions and type IIB superstring theory in a ten-dimensional geometry given by a product of a five-dimensional anti-de Sitter space (AdS5) and a five-dimensional sphere (S5). There are N units of f ive-form flux threading the five sphere. There are also analogous M-theory dualities. These dualities are sometimes referred to as AdS/CFT dualities. AdS stands for anti-de Sitter space, a maximally symmetric space-time geometry with negative scalar curvature. CFT stands for conformal field theory, a quantum field theory that is invariant under the group of conformal transformations. This type of equivalence is an example of a holographic duality, since it is analogous to representing three-dimensional space on a two-dimensional emulsion. The study of these dualities is teaching us a great deal about string theory and M-theory as well as the dual quantum f ield theories. String and M-theory cosmology The field of superstring cosmology is emerging as a new and exciting discipline. String theorists and string-theory considerations are injecting new ideas into the study of cosmology. This might be the arena in which predictions that are specific to string theory first confront data. In a quantum theory that contains gravity, such as string theory, the cosmological constant, Λ, which characterizes the energy density of the vacuum, is (at least in principle) a computable quantity. This energy (sometimes called dark energy) has recently been measured to fairly good accuracy, and found to account for about 70% of the total mass/energy in the present-day Universe. This fraction is an increasing function of time. The observed value of the cosmological constant/dark energy is important for cosmology, but it is extremely tiny when expressed in Planck units (about 10−120). The first attempts to account for $\Lambda > 0$ within string theory and M-theory, based on compactifying 11-dimensional supergravity on time-independent compact manifolds, were ruled out by "no-go" theorems. However, certain non perturbative effects allow these no-go theorems to be circumvented. A viewpoint that has gained in popularity recently is that string theory can accommodate almost any value of Λ, but only solutions for which Λ is sufficiently small describe a Universe that can support life. So, if it were much larger, we wouldn't be here to ask the question. This type of reasoning is called anthropic. While this may be correct, it would be satisfying to have another explanation of why Λ is so small that does not require this type of reasoning. Another important issue in cosmology concerns the accelerated expansion of the very early Universe, which is referred to as inflation. The observational case for inflation is quite strong, and it is an important question to understand how it arises from a fundamental theory. Before the period of inflation was the Big Bang, the origin of the observable Universe, and much effort is going into understanding that. Two radically different proposals are quantum tunneling from nothing and a collision of branes.

The Weirdness of String Theory

Quantum mechanics is a difficult subject to get your head around and the more you think you know about it, the more you discover you don't look much at all. There are many contradictions in physics yet all of them are meant to hold true. Take the Standard Model of quantum physics for example. It states that everything is made up of particles, but string theory disagrees. It says they're simply strings, each vibrating to their beat. Using the Standard Model again as a reference, it means there are 12 basic building blocks of the universe in the form of six quarks and six leptons. Included in this mixture are four fundamental forces: gravity, electromagnetism, and the strong and weak nuclear forces. Out of these four forces, the one that has scientists most puzzled is gravity. The reason for this is that the others are much easier to prove and arise from the exchange of an elementary particle. Photons impact the attraction of electromagnetism. Gluons bind the strong nuclear force, while W and Z bosons string the weak nuclear force together.

Regarding gravity, scientists have suggested a particle called the graviton could be responsible for gravity, but as of yet, are unable to prove its existence.

String Theory assumes we live in a universe with at least 10 dimensions. " The idea of dimensions may sound exciting, but they would cause real problems if you forget where you parked your car." – Stephen Hawking

However, string theory proposes that these elementary particles are simply different versions of a tiny loop of string that vibrate at different frequencies to create different kinds of particles. If the strings oscillate one way we may see a photon but oscillate in another way and we may see an electron. Once you accept this theory, it's quite easy to accept there's a kind of oscillation that creates a graviton. But, there are a few things that might make it harder, with the first being for string theory to work the universe needs to have ay least 10 dimensions. So why then do we only perceive four (up-down, forward-backward, right-left, and time)? One idea suggests it's because the other dimensions are tucked away and folded down in such a way that we can't see them. But as of yet, it is just a theory and until we have some concrete proof it will remain that way.

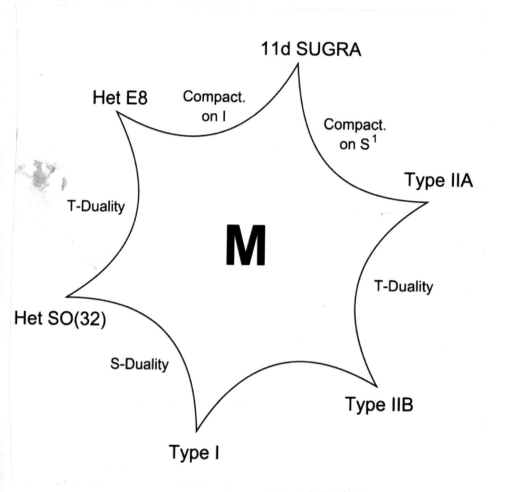

So when you ask me how string theory might be tested, I can tell you what's likely to happen at accelerators or some parts of the theory that are likely to be tested.

(Edward Witten)

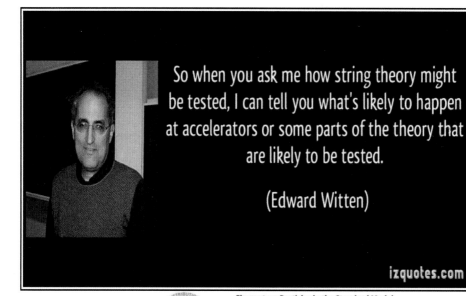

ATOM

NUCLEUS

PROTON

Made in United States
Orlando, FL
07 November 2022